DISCOVERING
THE
PROMISES
OF
God

Dr. Mark Cress
Dan Nelson *ILLUSTRATOR*

Discovering the Promises of God

by Dr. Mark Cress

Copyright © 2010 Lanphier Press

ISBN 978-1-934570-13-5

For Worldwide Distribution

Printed in the USA

Lanphier Press

USA

www.lanphierpress.com

Contents

ACKNOWLEDGEMENTS

More than fifteen years ago, God brought me into a wonderful relationship with my dear friend Dr. Dwayne Reece, the Vice President and General Manager of my publisher, Lanphier Press. Obviously, he was one of the first people I talked with about this project, after feeling certain God was calling and engaging me with this concept. Dwayne is a good and godly man with keen spiritual insights and plenty of street smarts. More than simply encouraging me, he immediately jumped at the chance to help me produce the work. In our initial conversation he actually gave me the perfect title... *Discovering the Promises of God*. More encouragement and good ideas quickly came from my precious friends, Jess Duboy, Jeff Hilles, and Ron Duke. Finally, as has been the case for more than three decades, my dear wife Linda offered support beyond belief. I pray God's richest blessings on everyone who helped with this little book in any way. First and foremost...my dear Jesus.

INTRODUCTION

Throughout the Bible, God offers definite and abundant promises. These promises He offers freely, yet some come with a great cost.

Theologians throughout the ages have documented well the fact that God deeply desires to communicate with us in two primary ways. One is through prayer and the other is through His divinely inspired Word... the Bible.

For nearly two decades, God has allowed us to serve employees through the mission outreach of Corporate Chaplains of America. Now, with fellow chaplains serving alongside me from coast to coast, the need for God's direct intervention in the lives of His creation has never been clearer.

Each and every day, we all need to hear from God. We need to hear Him speak directly into our lives. We desperately need to feel His presence in our lives... not just week by week, but literally hour by hour, minute by minute and second by second.

In the Bible, God makes some astonishing claims and promises that contain the power to literally trans-

9

form our lives. When we listen to God's promises and actually speak them back to Him in prayer, our lives can be changed forever.

This little book is simply a collection of God's promises designed to empower you to connect with God in a deep and abiding way...hopefully, as never before.

I asked my dear friend, Dan Nelson, who just happens to be one of the most talented Christian artists of our time, to very simply illustrate in charcoal how God speaks to him through each of the promises. As you turn each page, on the right you will encounter God's promise and on the left, how God used it to speak to Dan through his artistic talent.

Start now by asking God, in prayer, to speak to you directly through His promises printed on these pages. Ask Him to change your life. Ask Him for guidance. Talk to Him about your dreams and goals. Claim His promises as your own and watch your life change forever.

As you continue to read your Bible and communicate with God each day, never forget to claim the promises of a great and loving God. He truly wants the very best for us. He loves us so much that He sacrificed His only Son, Jesus, in order for us to be redeemed from the life of sin we inherited from our original brother, Adam, at the beginning of time. The very first promise He gives us, as new believers, is to indwell us with the power of His Holy Spirit. If you have never surrendered yourself fully to God by accepting Jesus as Lord and by asking Him to forgive you of your sins…now would be a great time to do so. Just bow your head and talk to God. Ask Him to come into your life and change you right now. Tell Him you are sorry for your sins and truly desire His forgiveness. Ask Him to show you the way and guide your paths until you are united with Him in Heaven, someday in the future. He promises to redeem you and fill you with a life more abundant than you might ever expect.

Maybe you have been a Christian for some time and simply need to re-connect with God in a new and refreshing way. Why not start here in prayer by asking God to make good on His promise to renew His Holy Spirit in your life. Regardless of your tenure as a believer…by all means…discover the promises of God and be transformed…starting now!

COURAGE

chapter 1

HAVE I not
commanded you?
Be strong and of
good courage;
do not be afraid,
nor be dismayed,
for the LORD your
God is with you
wherever you go."

Joshua 1:9

BE strong and of good courage, and do it; do not fear nor be dismayed, for the LORD God – my God – will be with you. He will not leave you nor forsake you..."

1 Chronicles 28:20

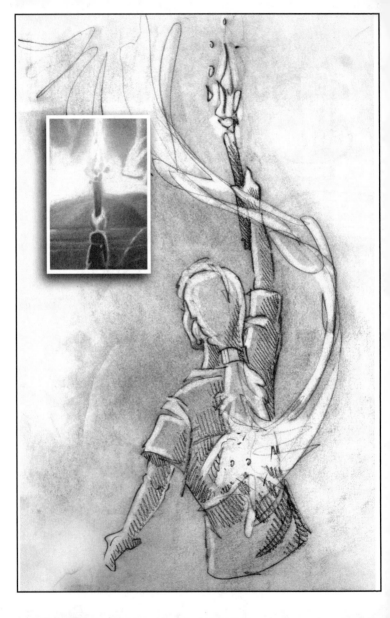

"BE of good courage, and He shall strengthen your heart, all you who hope in the LORD."

Psalm 31:24

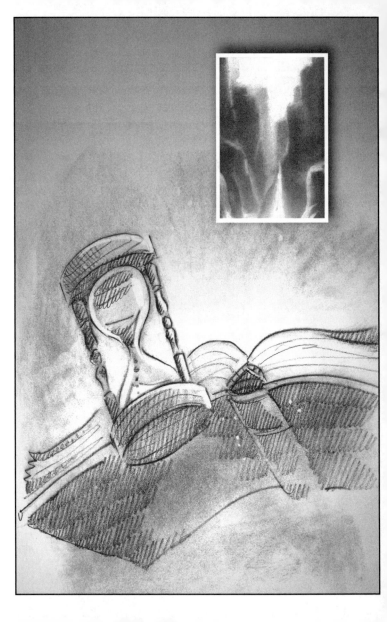

WAIT on the LORD; be of good courage, and He shall strengthen your heart; wait, I say, on the LORD!"

Psalm 27:14

E strong and of good courage, do not fear nor be afraid of them; for the LORD your God, He is the One who goes with you. He will not leave you nor forsake you."

Deuteronomy 31:6

 give them eternal life, and they shall never perish; neither shall anyone snatch them out of My hand. My Father, who has given them to Me, is greater than all; and no one is able to snatch them out of My Father's hand."

John 10:28-29

"WATCH, stand fast in the faith, be brave, be strong. Let all that you do be done with love."

1 Corinthians 16:13-14

GRIEF

chapter 2

BUT I would
strengthen you
with my mouth, and
the comfort of my lips
would relieve your
grief."

Job 16:5

THEREFORE you
now have sorrow;
but I will see you again
and your heart will
rejoice, and your joy
no one will take from
you."

John 16:22

"TROUBLE and anguish have overtaken me, yet Your commandments are my delights."

Psalm 119:143

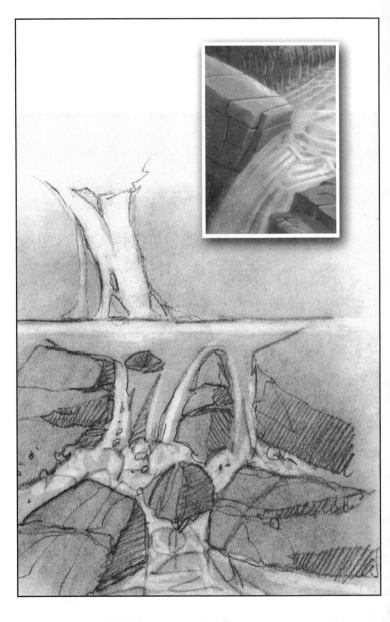

"THE blessing of the LORD makes one rich, And He adds no sorrow with it."

Proverbs 10:22

"Do not sorrow, for the joy of the LORD is your strength."

Nehemiah 8:10b

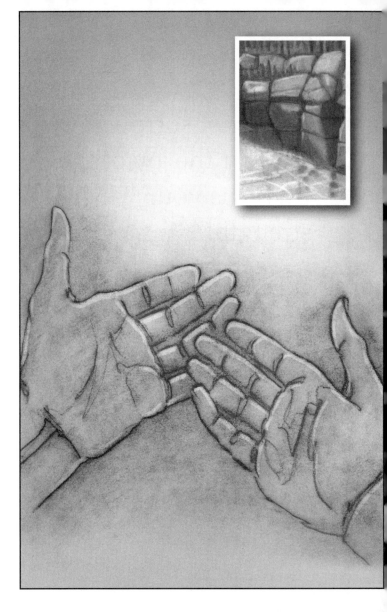

"FOR the Lord will not cast off forever. Though He causes grief, yet He will show compassion according to the multitude of His mercies."

Lamentations 3:31-32

WORRY & ANXIETY

chapter 3

THEREFORE I say to you, do not worry about your life, what you will eat or what you will drink; nor about your body, what you will put on. Is not life more than food and the body more than clothing?"

Matthew 6:25

THEREFORE do not worry, saying, 'What shall we eat?' or 'What shall we drink?' or 'What shall we wear?' For after all these things the Gentiles seek. For your heavenly Father knows that you need all these things.
But seek first the kingdom of God and His righteousness, and all these things shall be added to you."

Matthew 6:31-33

BUT when they deliver you up, do not worry about how or what you should speak. For it will be given to you in that hour what you should speak; for it is not you who speak, but the Spirit of your Father who speaks in you."

Matthew 10:19-20

BE anxious for nothing, but in everything by prayer and supplication, with thanksgiving, let your requests be made known to God; and the peace of God, which surpasses all understanding, will guard your hearts and minds through Christ Jesus."

Philippians 4:6-7

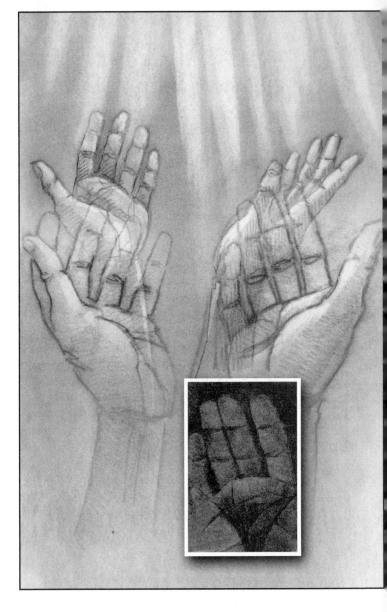

THEREFORE humble yourselves under the mighty hand of God, that He may exalt you in due time, casting all your care upon Him, for He cares for you."

I Peter 5:6-7

THEREFORE do not worry about tomorrow, for tomorrow will worry about its own things. Sufficient for the day is its own trouble."

Matthew 6:34

TRUST in the LORD with all your heart, and lean not on your own understanding; in all your ways acknowledge Him, and He shall direct your paths."

Proverbs 3:5-6

HOPE

chapter 4

GOD is able to make all grace abound toward you, that you, always having all sufficiency in all things, may have an abundance for every good work."

2 Corinthians 9:8

BEHOLD, the eye of the LORD is on those who fear Him, On those who hope in His mercy."

Psalm 33:18

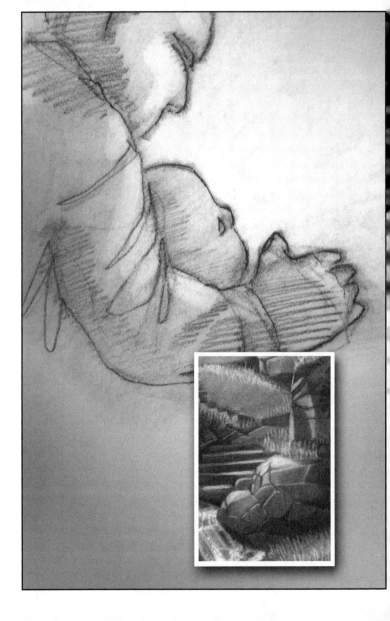

FOR You are my
hope, O Lord
GOD; You are my
trust from my youth."

Psalm 71:5

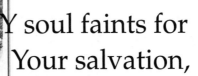

My soul faints for
Your salvation,
but I hope in Your
word."

Psalm 119:81

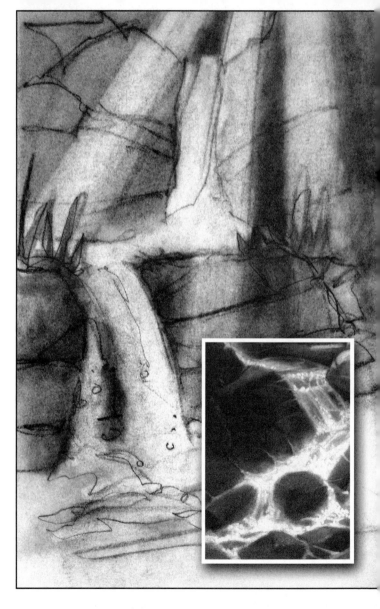

FOR I know the thoughts that I think toward you, says the LORD, thoughts of peace and not of evil, to give you a future and a hope."

Jeremiah 29:11

NOW may the God of hope fill you with all joy and peace in believing, that you may abound in hope by the power of the Holy Spirit."

Romans 15:13

HAPPY is he who
has the God of
Jacob for his help,
whose hope is in the
LORD his God, Who
made heaven and
earth, the sea, and all
that is in them; Who
keeps truth forever."

Psalm 146:5-6

Dan Nelson

LOSS

chapter 5

ET not your heart
be troubled; you
believe in God, believe
also in Me. In My Father's
house are many mansions; if
it were not so, I would have
told you. I go to prepare a
place for you. And if I go and
prepare a place for you, I will
come again and receive you
to Myself; that where I am,
there you may be also."

John 14:1-3

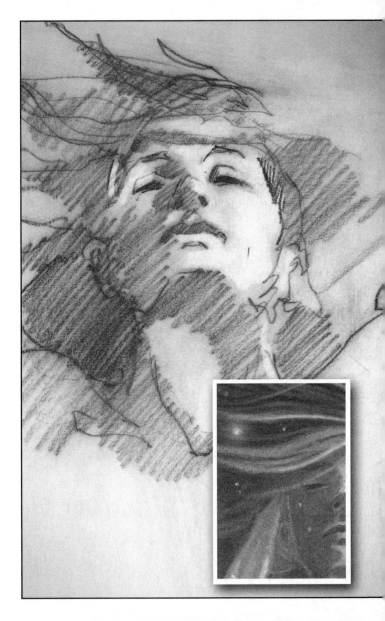

*A*ND God will wipe away every tear from their eyes; there shall be no more death, nor sorrow, nor crying. There shall be no more pain, for the former things have passed away."

Revelation 21:4

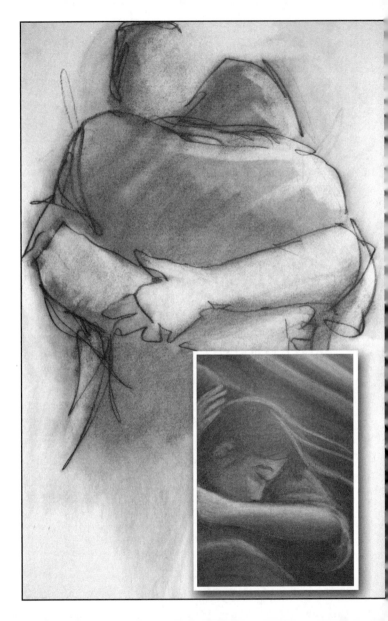

BLESSED are those
who mourn, for
they shall be
comforted."

Matthew 5:4

PRECIOUS in the sight of the LORD is the death of His saints."

Psalm 116:15

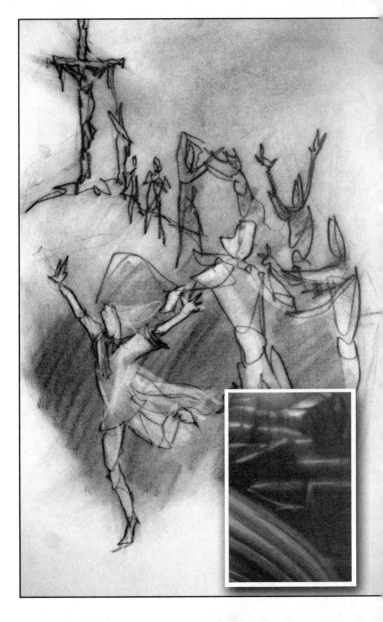

"FOR God did not appoint us to wrath, but to obtain salvation through our Lord Jesus Christ, who died for us, that whether we wake or sleep, we should live together with Him. Therefore comfort each other and edify one another, just as you also are doing."

1 Thessalonians 5:9-11

WHY are you cast down, O my soul? And why are you disquieted within me? Hope in God, for I shall yet praise Him for the help of His countenance."

Psalm 42:5

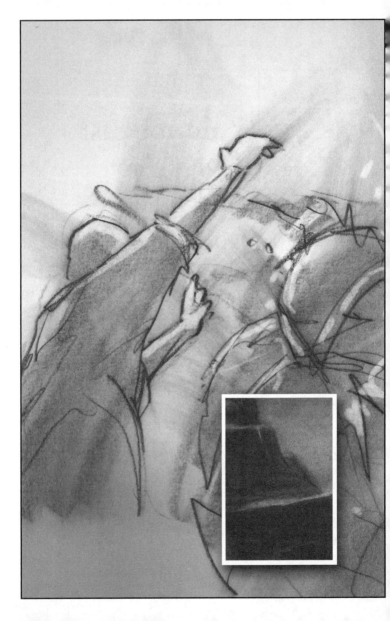

CAST your burden on the LORD, and He shall sustain you; He shall never permit the righteous to be moved."

Psalm 55:22

THEREFORE we do not lose heart. Even though our outward man is perishing, yet the inward man is being renewed day by day. For our light affliction, which is but for a moment, is working for us a far more exceeding and eternal weight of glory, while we do not look at the things which are seen, but at the things which are not seen. For the things which are seen are temporary, but the things which are not seen are eternal."

2 Corinthians 4:16-18

LONELINESS

chapter 6

A man who has friends must himself be friendly, but there is a friend who sticks closer than a brother."

Proverbs 18:24

WHEN my father and my mother forsake me, then the LORD will take care of me."

Psalm 27:10

FOR He Himself has said, 'I will never leave you nor forsake you' so we may boldly say: 'The LORD is my helper; I will not fear. What can man do to me?'"

Hebrews 13:5b-6

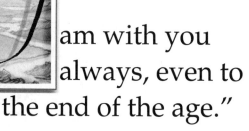 am with you
always, even to
the end of the age."

Matthew 28:20b

FOR the LORD will not forsake His people, for His great name's sake, because it has pleased the LORD to make you His people."

1 Samuel 12:22

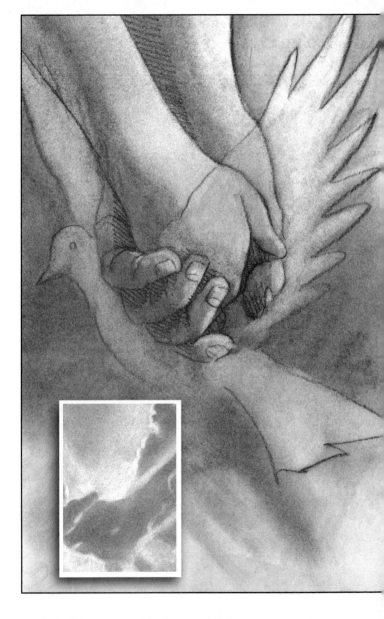

 will not leave
you orphans;
I will come to you."

John 14:18

FOR I am persuaded
that neither death
nor life, nor angels nor
principalities nor powers, nor
things present nor things to
come, nor height nor depth,
nor any other created thing,
shall be able to separate us
from the love of God which
is in Christ Jesus our Lord."

Romans 8:38-39

PEACE

chapter 7

THESE things I have spoken to you, that in Me you may have peace. In the world you will have tribulation; but be of good cheer, I have overcome the world."

John 16:33

"I will both lie
down in peace,
and sleep; For You
alone, O LORD, make
me dwell in safety."

Psalm 4:8

YOU will keep him in perfect peace, whose mind is stayed on You, because he trusts in You. Trust in the LORD forever, for in YAH, the LORD, is everlasting strength."

Isaiah 26:3-4

"HE shall enter into peace; they shall rest in their beds, each one walking in his uprightness."

Isaiah 57:2

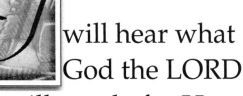

I will hear what God the LORD will speak, for He will speak peace To His people and to His saints."

Psalm 85:8

FOR to be carnally minded is death, but to be spiritually minded is life and peace."

Romans 8:6

NOW acquaint yourself with Him, and be at peace; thereby good will come to you."

Job 22:21

WISDOM

chapter 8

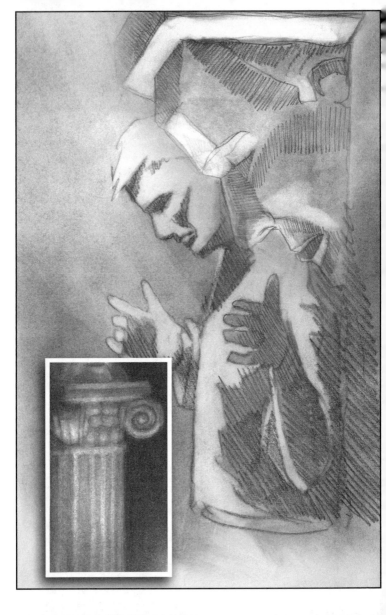

THE fear of the LORD is the beginning of wisdom, and the knowledge of the Holy One is understanding."

Proverbs 9:10

*I*F any of you lacks wisdom, let him ask of God, who gives to all liberally and without reproach, and it will be given to him."

James 1:5

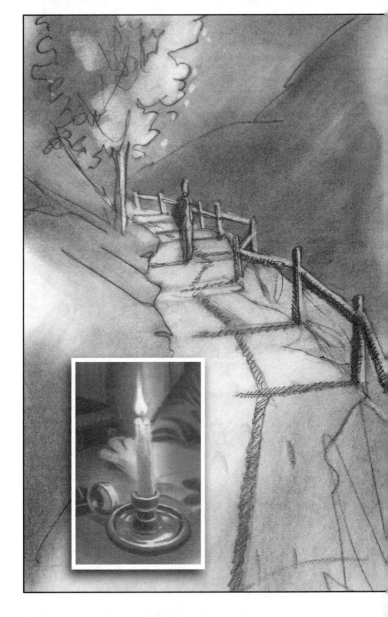

THE fear of the LORD is the beginning of wisdom; a good understanding have all those who do His commandments. His praise endures forever."

Psalm 111:10

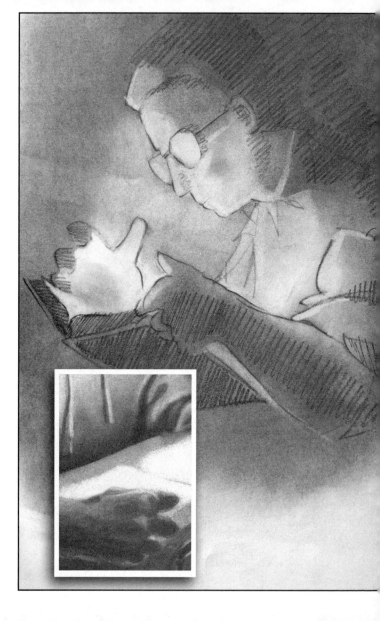

WISDOM is the principal thing; therefore get wisdom. And in all your getting, get understanding."

Proverbs 4:7

"TEACH me good judgment and knowledge, for I believe Your commandments."

Psalm 119:66

WHOEVER loves instruction loves knowledge, but he who hates correction is stupid."

Proverbs 12:1

FOR God gives wisdom and knowledge and joy to a man who is good in His sight; but to the sinner He gives the work of gathering and collecting, that he may give to him who is good before God. This also is vanity and grasping for the wind."

Ecclesiastes 2:26

FEAR

chapter 9

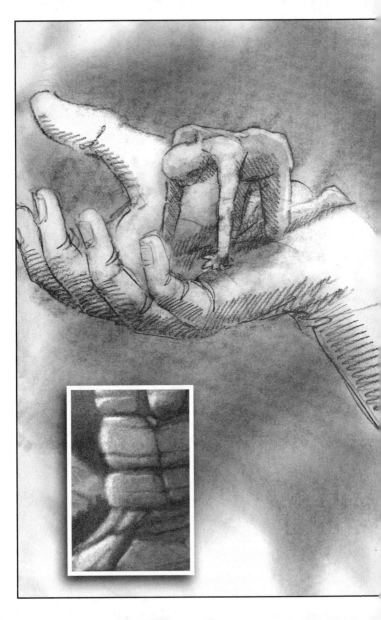

FEAR not, for I am with you; be not dismayed, for I am your God. I will strengthen you, yes, I will help you, I will uphold you with My righteous right hand."

Isaiah 41:10

PEACE I leave with you, My peace I give to you; not as the world gives do I give to you. Let not your heart be troubled, neither let it be afraid."

John 14:27

GOD is our refuge and strength, a very present help in trouble. Therefore we will not fear, even though the earth be removed, and though the mountains be carried into the midst of the sea; though its waters roar and be troubled, though the mountains shake with its swelling."

Psalm 46:1-3

So we may boldly say: 'The LORD is my helper; I will not fear' what can man do to me."

Hebrews 13:6

AND do not fear those who kill the body but cannot kill the soul. But rather fear Him who is able to destroy both soul and body in hell."

Matthew 10:28

THERE is no fear in love; but perfect love casts out fear, because fear involves torment. But he who fears has not been made perfect in love."

1 John 4:18

OR you did not receive the spirit of bondage again to fear, but you received the Spirit of adoption by whom we cry out, Abba, Father."

Romans 8:15

STRESS

chapter 10

OME to Me, all you who labor and are heavy laden, and I will give you rest. Take My yoke upon you and learn from Me, for I am gentle and lowly in heart, and you will find rest for your souls."

Matthew 11:28-29

WE are hard-pressed on every side, yet not crushed; we are perplexed, but not in despair; persecuted, but not forsaken; struck down, but not destroyed — always carrying about in the body the dying of the Lord Jesus, that the life of Jesus also may be manifested in our body."

2 Corinthians 4:8-10

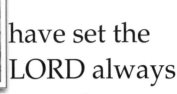

"I have set the
LORD always
before me; because He
is at my right hand I
shall not be moved."

Psalm 16:8

"IN my distress I called upon the LORD, and cried out to my God; He heard my voice from His temple, and my cry entered His ears."

2 Samuel 22:7

AND He said, 'My Presence will go with you, and I will give you rest."

Exodus 33:14

"I will both lie down in peace, and sleep; for You alone, O LORD, make me dwell in safety."

Psalm 4:8

THE righteous cry out, and the LORD hears, and delivers them out of all their troubles. The LORD is near to those who have a broken heart, and saves such as have a contrite spirit."

Psalm 34:17-18

WORK & FINANCES

chapter 11

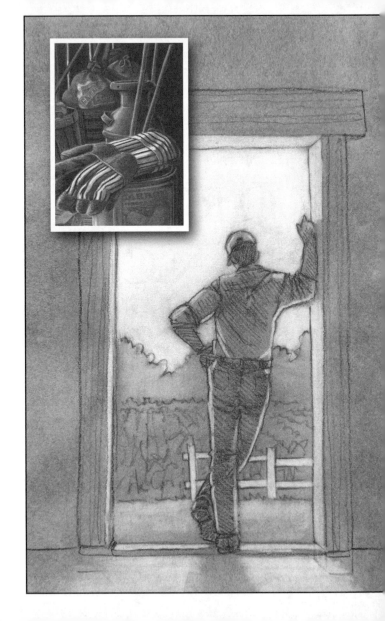

"**G**ODLINESS with contentment is great gain."

1 Timothy 6:6

THERE is one who makes himself rich, yet has nothing; and one who makes himself poor, yet has great riches."

Proverbs 13:7

OMMAND those who are rich in this present age not to be haughty, nor to trust in uncertain riches but in the living God, who gives us richly all things to enjoy."

1 Timothy 6:17

IN all labor there is profit, but idle chatter leads only to poverty."

Proverbs 14:23

HE who loves silver will not be satisfied with silver; nor he who loves abundance, with increase. This also is vanity."

Ecclesiastes 5:10

"GIVE and it will be given to you: good measure, pressed down, shaken together, and running over will be put into your bosom. For with the same measure that you use, it will be measured back to you."

Luke 6:38

AND whatever you do, do it heartily, as to the Lord and not to men, knowing that from the Lord you will receive the reward of the inheritance; for you serve the Lord Christ."

Colossians 3:23-24

JOY

chapter 12

THIS is the day the LORD has made; we will rejoice and be glad in it."

Psalm 118:24

I know also, my God, that You test the heart and have pleasure in uprightness. As for me, in the uprightness of my heart I have willingly offered all these things; and now with joy I have seen Your people, who are present here to offer willingly to You."

1 Chronicles 29:17

RESTORE to me the joy of Your salvation, and uphold me by Your generous Spirit."

Psalm 51:12

I say to you that likewise there will be more joy in heaven over one sinner who repents than over ninety-nine just persons who need no repentance."

Luke 15:7

BUT now I come
to You, and these
things I speak in the
world, that they may
have My joy fulfilled
in themselves."

John 17:13

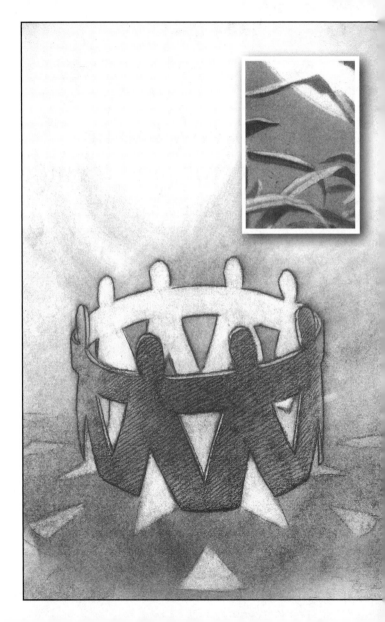

THEREFORE if there is any consolation in Christ, if any comfort of love, if any fellowship of the Spirit, if any affection and mercy, fulfill my joy by being like-minded, having the same love, being of one accord, of one mind."

Philippians 2:1-2

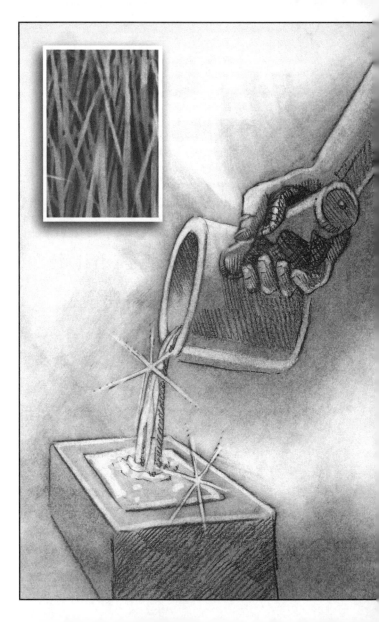

$\mathcal{M}$Y brethren, count it all joy when you fall into various trials, knowing that the testing of your faith produces patience."

James 1:2-3

THE ULTIMATE PROMISE

"FOR the wages of sin is death, but the gift of God is eternal life in Christ Jesus our Lord."

Romans 6:23

The ultimate promise God makes to every human being is the promise we most need to hear. Romans 6:23 details God's promise to pay the penalty for our sin and give us the gift of eternal life through Jesus' death on the cross. If you have never surrendered yourself fully to God by accepting Jesus as Lord and asking Him to forgive you of your sins...now would be a great time to do so. Simply bow your head and talk with God.

Dear Lord Jesus,

I know that I am a sinner, and I ask for Your forgiveness. I believe You died for my sins and rose from the dead. I turn from my sins and invite You to come into my heart and life. I want to trust and follow You as my Lord and Savior.

In Your Name, Amen.

_____

Signature

_____

Date

WHAT DAN SAW IN HIS MIND AS GOD SPOKE TO HIM THROUGH EACH VERSE

As friends and colleagues reviewed the rough drafts of this project, many would ask about Dan's inspiration for some of his art relative to certain verses of Scripture. Week by week as we continued to work on the project, I began to ask Dan this question and became fascinated with how God truly seemed to be working with him through his art. At this point, it seemed only natural to have Dan offer a single statement for each drawing to help us gain insight for each piece of his work.

COURAGE

Courage 1 – It was actually the pre-incarnate Jesus who accompanied the people of God throughout the Old Testament. See 1 Corinthians 10:4.

Courage 2 – The four letter Hebrew name of God (Y-H-W-H) is depicted as a fiery "swoosh" from heaven enveloping and protecting the young warrior.

Courage 3 – The Spirit of God infuses and enlightens the heart of this pilgrim.

Courage 4 – Waiting on the Lord suggests time spent in intimate communion with Him and in the Scriptures.

Courage 5 – The strong hand of the Lord always interposes between us and our enemies – visible and invisible. See Psalm 5:11-12.

Courage 6 – When we follow the Lord, it is not just we, ourselves, who reap the benefit. We are strong for "our people"– family, friends, and associates.

Courage 7 – When we stand in the Lord, we stand shoulder-to-shoulder with our brothers and sisters all over the world. See 1 Peter 5:9.

GRIEF

Grief 1 – God often uses the peacefulness of nature to comfort us in times of grief.

Grief 2 – The Holy Spirit breathes life and comfort into us through the words of Scripture.

Grief 3 – The joy that Jesus gives is as expansive and eternal as a sunburst above clouds.

Grief 4 – The water in a rippling brook is purified even as it tumbles over the rocks. There is no "sorrow" mixed with it.

Grief 5 – The Scriptures often speak of one's "horn" being lifted up – the image of a bull or stag exulting in his indomitable strength. See Psalm 92:10

Grief 6 – A familiar image comes to mind as we contemplate God's compassion and mercy: ". . . Underneath are the everlasting arms." (Deuteronomy 33:27 KJV)

WORRY AND ANXIETY

Worry 1 – A rainbow – the ultimate symbol of God's hope – infuses our being with light and life, and then flows out of us as "rivers of living water."

Worry 2 – Is that a mountain or a castle? As we lift our eyes to seek His Kingdom, all lesser concerns fade into insignificance.

Worry 3 – Stone walls are transformed by the Holy Spirit into a sanctuary filled with peace.

Worry 4 – We give our concerns to God . . . and He shelters our hearts in the sanctuary of His presence.

Worry 5 – Through lifted hands we give our cares to the Lord, then receive assurance of His love.

Worry 6 – Each day will have its challenges, but worrying about them does no good, and only ruins the peace of the moment.

Worry 7 – The Lord accompanies us on the path of life... and puts guardrails where we need them.

HOPE

Hope 1 – The water of a fountain doesn't just trickle out, it springs out in abundance. Notice at all the "alls" of this fountain - like promise.

Hope 2 – Sun-rays from the sky and an aerial view of a home convey the sense that God looks upon us with great affection and care.

Hope 3 – One of the most poignant images we possess of God's love is that of being held like a small child in our Father's lap.

Hope 4 – To climb is to hope; we "faint" for more of God because we have every expectation of achieving what we faint for – a higher level of relationship with Him.

Hope 5 – A thundering waterfall never dries up; the Lord's thoughts toward us are unceasing and full of joyful expectation.

Hope 6 – A great oak tree conveys the power of the Holy Spirit giving us a sure foundation of hope.

Hope 7 – A light house by the sea is the perfect image of help and hope in the midst of life's storms.

LOSS

Loss 1 – Jesus, the Carpenter of the Ages, welcomes us to the home He has built for us.

Loss 2 – This face reflects the unadulterated bliss promised in this verse: Nothing bad . . . forever.

Loss 3 – We are not merely comforted, but comforted by a perfect Father.

Loss 4 – In death the believer is actually taken up... with God and into His glory.

Loss 5 – The redemption of the entire cosmos flows from the amazing cross of Calvary. So Paul says, "Let us celebrate!" (1 Corinthians 5:8 NLT)

Loss 6 – Even in moments of discouragement we can tell our souls what to do: Hope in God! And in the hoping we are released into the light.

Loss 7 – Even after we cast off our heavy burdens, the Lord promises to hold us up and make us unmovable.

Loss 8 – Light and flight! What better way to indicate the glory that will be ours in the next life?

LONELINESS

Loneliness 1 – Jesus shows up best in the midst of friendship.

Loneliness 2 – The chair of a loved one may be empty, but the light of God's presence still infuses us.

Loneliness 3 – In the Hebrew Scriptures, the image of crashing waves is often a reference to the nations rebelling against God and his people. See Psalm 65:7.

Loneliness 4 – The river of time stretches into eternity . . . and Jesus is with us at every turn.

Loneliness 5 – He is pleased to be our Shepherd . . . even when we are sometimes dumb sheep.

Loneliness 6 – Jesus has indeed come to us through the Holy Spirit, and we are held both in Jesus' hands and the Father's hands. See John 10: 28-29.

Loneliness 7 – Living in the shadow of the cross–the ultimate proof of God's love– makes us invincible in this life.

PEACE

Peace 1 – A child can sleep in peace without a care in the world.

Peace 2 – Sleep as restful as the hills – now that's a good prospect!

Peace 3 – The figure rests peacefully in this scene because of the strength of the tree, the symbol of God's strength.

Peace 4 – Warm light streaming from cozy bedroom windows – an image of utter peace and quietness.

Peace 5 – Since it is hard to indicate that someone is singing in a drawing, the lullaby is changed into a flute. See Zephaniah 3:17.

Peace 6 – A flower represents life; in this case, the flower is a peace lily. So we have life and peace in the flower... and perhaps spiritual-mindedness in the butterfly.

Peace 7 – Light represents revelation from God; glasses, the capacity to receive that revelation; and the Bible a primary means of gaining our acquaintance with Him.

WISDOM

Wisdom 1 – This receptive man receives wisdom and is morphed into a pillar – even a pillar of wisdom. See Proverbs 9:1.

Wisdom 2 – The pitcher is a symbol of generous giving. Wisdom is not so much something we get as something God gives.

Wisdom 3 – Commandments are sometimes compared to "guardrails"; they keep us from going into danger.

Wisdom 4 – Wisdom and understanding are "light" to our souls.

Wisdom 5 – Good judgment is the ability to make good decisions.

Wisdom 6 – Knowledge doesn't lead to wisdom, but wisdom does lead to a love of knowledge. See 1 Kings 4:33.

Wisdom 7 – It is easy for us to see a young child as "good." And that is exactly how our Father sees us.

Wisdom 8 – We actually have the capacity to share with God the wisdom He exercised in creating the universe.

FEAR

Fear 1 – To be held in God's hand is the most secure place in the universe.

Fear 2 – Rowing across a calm lake at sunset... His promises help get our souls to that place.

Fear 3 – A castle is a familiar image of refuge and strength. No matter what is going on on the outside, there is peace within.

Fear 4 – Behind the protection of God's redemptive shield we are bold and fearless warriors.

Fear 5 – Our confidence is not in the natural instruments of self-protection, our confidence is in the One who holds our life in His hands.

Fear 6 – Like a small child holding a pet, there is no fear in love.

Fear 7 – The perfect picture of our adopted state–the love of a father for his young child.

STRESS
Stress 1 – A good saddle fits; a good horse trusts his master.
Stress 2 – Effective people put themselves in challenging places every day. Sustained by the life of Jesus we can face hardship and adversity without fear.
Stress 3 – This cowboy faces the Light... and even his Bible is at his right hand.
Stress 4 – Huge clouds remind us of God's amazing condescension to hear our prayers.
Stress 5 – In the shadow of the mare the foal is at rest.
Stress 6 – Wagons in the old west were circled for safety. In that context even a child could play without stress.
Stress 7 – This cowboy represents a contrite spirit. The presence of his faithful horse suggests the deliverance God promises.

WORK AND FINANCES
Work and Finances 1 – Farmers are the perfect picture of hard work and patient waiting. See James 5:7.

Work and Finances 2 – Riches are measured in many things; peace, love, and joy, among them.

Work and Finances 3 – Most of the sketches in this book show the positive side of each promise. This is the one rare exception. Here "uncertain riches" have crashed.

Work and Finances 4 – Even the smallest effort yields some benefit– from a bountiful visible harvest to the simple contentment of a job well-done.

Work and Finances 5 – Opulent wealth and bored youth are often found together.

Work and Finances 6 – We receive from the Lord more than we could ever give away.

Work and Finances 7 – We will receive the reward of a job well-done – both in this life and the next.

JOY

Joy 1 – These are day lilies – rejoicing in the morning sun.

Joy 2 – In this passage, David rejoices at the sight of God's people worshipping the Lord.

Joy 3 – The Hebrew word for "Spirit" is the same as the word for "wind". This person is almost being lifted off their feet by the "wind of the Spirit".

Joy 4 – The joy of heaven shines down on this repentant person.

Joy 5 – To have Jesus' very own joy filling us would make us as carefree as a child playing in the waves under the loving eyes of her parents.

Joy 6 – This pictograph illustrates the essence of our fellowship –our "one-accord-ness" – in Christ.

Joy 7 – A familiar symbol of faith is that of refined gold. See 1 Peter 1:7.

ABOUT THE AUTHOR

Mark Cress is Founder & CEO of Corporate Chaplains of America (*www.chaplain.org*), an organization whose mission is to build caring relationships with the hope of gaining permission to share the life-changing Good News of Jesus Christ, in a non-threatening manner.

Mark is a life-long entrepreneur and CEO of more than 25 years. He holds two business degrees, a Master of Divinity degree, and a doctorate in Leadership and Business Ethics and is the author of five books.

Mark and his wife of 30 years, Linda, reside in North Carolina and have two happily married adult daughters.

ABOUT THE ILLUSTRATOR

Dan Nelson has always been a full-time artist. Dan Nelson has always been in full-time ministry. That's the easiest way to put it.

He holds a Bachelor's degree in Fine Arts from Calvin College and a Master of Divinity from Southwestern Baptist Theological Seminary, but his real education has come over 35 years serving as artist-and-youth pastor, artist-and-worship leader and as artist-and-church planter.

To learn more about Dan's work, visit him at *www.DanNelsonArt.com*.

Dan and Nancy live in Raleigh, North Carolina, have been happily married for 30 years, and have four mostly-grown (wonderful) children.

ADDITIONAL RESOURCES FROM LANPHIER PRESS

The Third Awakening
Print or Audio Book available of this title. This is a fast, fun novel of intrigue and romance that shows how the Holy Spirit works in the lives of ordinary people and how, through them, a third great awakening may occur. Follow the story of how BB, his grandmother, wife, and friends travel to a place they never expected to reach and what happened to their plans. (131 pages hardcover; also available in Spanish)

Twenty Words that Will Change Your Life Forever
Ten workbooks with one audio facilitator CD for small groups. (Can also be ordered in 5 packs or individually) The author reveals ten "Core Values" that, properly applied, can truly change your life forever. Used solo, or as a group devotional, this resource has the ability to help you make genuine changes that will last for eternity.

The Compass

If you have ever asked the question, "What is available for my new Christian friend to help him or her get started on the right foot as a genuine believer?", *The Compass* is exactly what you have been looking for. *The Compass*, with its high impact DVD, audio CD, and 48-page book-

let, introduces the believer to all aspects of their new walk with the Lord. This innovative kit immerses the user in the five basic fundamentals of a serious Christian walk.

C-Change

The real life story of a committed chaplain who spends his days making a difference in the lives of every

employee he encounters. The author brings great wit, as well as real life chaplain and CEO experience, to the book that allows the reader to experience the action of a chaplain on a very personal level, while at the same time imparting leadership principles that can make a real dif-

ference. Print or Audio Book available of this title.

Discovering the Promises of God
If this book has impacted your life we would enjoy hearing from you. Please contact us and share your story at: *impact@discoveringthepromises.org*.

You may order additional copies of this book individually or in discounted case quantities by visiting *www.discoveringthepromises.org* or *www.lanphierpress.com*.

Discovering the Promises of God is also available to other Biblically-based, Christ focused ministries for private labeling opportunities. Please contact *info@discoveringthepromises.org* to learn more.

www.discoveringthepromises.org
www.lanphierpress.com